Seeds of Hope

Walking through life from your

Scars → Stars

Sourness → Sweetness

Tears → Triumph

Test → Testimony

Lemons → Lemonade

Pain → Purpose

Felicia S.

QUEEN DREAM
PUBLISHING

" You think it, We ink it "

Seeds of Hope
Copyright © 2014 by Felicia S.
Illustrator: Ms. Reyes

All rights reserved. No part of this book may be reproduced or transmitted in any form or by any means without written permission from the author and Queen Dream Publishing.

ISBN: 978-0-9851433-2-9
Library of Congress Control: 17666441061
Printed in the United States of America

"Scriptures taken from the Holy Bible®."
Disclaimer:

Although the author and publisher have made every effort to ensure the accuracy & completeness of information presented in this book, we assume no responsibility for errors, inaccuracies, omissions, or any inconsistency herein. Any slights of people, places, or organizations are unintentional.

Author's Autograph Page

To:

From:

-Felicia S.

My message and ministry came from my mess; therefore, my personal motto is, "I will *listen* to, *encourage* and *pray* for others as well."

"Celebrate your future."

Dedication

I dedicate this vessel of hope to us both: you and I. I say that because as I minister in this book to you, help facilitate healing, infuse inspiration, plant encouragement, and seek God with you, I also minister, help, heal, inspire, encourage, and seek God for myself. I'd never speak to you from a platform that I can't relate to. That would be my opinion only, and I use God's opinion more than my own. Let's walk this out together. A wise man once said, "If you can't feel, then you can't heal." I have felt and I have been able to listen to others without judgment while they heal also. In life we are all a work in progress and imperfect creatures. If for any reason you consider yourself a perfect person, then stop reading here as this book is not for you. This book is for us, those that need God's constant hand, love, and support.

Special Dedication

A special dedication to my Aunt Ruby D. Murphy, may you rest in peace. Your daily emails and ministry of seeds of hope, scriptures you sent us all, like yourself will never be forgotten.

Honorary Dedications to the "Three Wise Men"

I pay tribute to the many sermons and leadership of numerous pastors and ministry leaders abroad. In particular, I salute three particular pastors, one in which is my current pastor of my church in Austell, GA. Another, my former pastor of a church where I served as a Stephen Minister in Houston, TX and another in Dallas, TX where this pastors televangelist ministry found me in the darkest of days in 2002. As a result of being active members of their heaven-sent congregations, these three pastors, as I have been growing as a Christian, have continuously planted *seeds of hope* in my life. I view their wisdom as though it comes directly from the three wise men in the Bible. Their divine interventions and leadership have been the breath of life and wisdom from above on many occasions. As they've been regular participants in my growth in life, I share their wisdom here and there sporadically throughout this vessel of light where needed in the form of *Seeds of Hope* with you also.

Table of Contents

Dedication	4
Special Dedication	4
Honorary Dedication	5
Prayer	7
Chapter: Seeds of Hope Intro	9
Chapter 1: Seeds of Encouragement	12
Chapter 2: Seeds for Love and Relationships	46
Chapter 3: Seeds for Friendships	70
Chapter 4: Seeds of Inspiration	84
Chapter 5: Seeds for Salvation	118
Chapter 6: Seeds to Go	151
Special Acknowledgements	156
Meet the Author	157

Join me in prayer…

"Forget the former things; do not dwell on the past. See I am doing a new thing! Now it springs up; do you not perceive it? I am making a way in the desert and streams in the wasteland."

—Isaiah 43:18-19

God can and will do a new thing.

Lord, have your way and your will in our life and those who read this book. Feed our faith; flush out our fear and any form of doubts. Protect us from and let us not associate, affiliate, or connect with those who plan to harm, hurt, or hinder us while we run this race called life. Lord, let us look straight while we run this race, only looking to our left or right to see what you have in our sight. We thank you that in our sight there are divine appointments, connections, and those you've called us to be with during this journey. Life is a journey and yes, Lord, let it be full of your will and your way for us. In the irreplaceable name of Jesus I pray, amen.

AIM High In Life

We all should strive to ***A. I. M.***

Abide In Me

"If you abide in Me, and My words abide in you, ask whatever you wish, and it will be done for you. My Father is glorified by this, that you bear much fruit, and so prove to be My disciples. Just as the Father has loved Me, I have also loved you; abide in My love."

——*John 15:7-9*

Introduction

Germination is a process. To grow anything worthy takes time and is a noted process. Whether growing plants, flowers, fruits, or vegetables, the germination process revolves around the right timing and soil, but most profoundly, the right seed.

Seeds of Hope is a semblance of seeds, whether it's a seed of encouragement, words of expressions, or simply a seed of inspiration. During the germination process, you can't hover over the seed you just have to do your part by maintaining the seed during the process. You have to leave the seed, water it occasionally, and trust God that it will grow right. It may wither, grow slowly, and appear as if it isn't growing at all, but know that it will grow left at times, or maybe grow right at other times, but have faith throughout the germination process that growth is inevitable. Trust the process. In other words, you can't control all situations. Trust God for the process while you live in faith. We reap what we sow *(Galatians 6:7)*. Sow the right seeds!

*Sowing **seeds** is Biblical, not an opinion.*

"A farmer went out to sow his seed. As he was scattering the seed, some fell along the path; it was trampled on and the birds of the air ate it up. Some fell on rock, and when it came up, the plants withered because they had no moisture. Other seed fell among thorns, which grew up with it and choked the plants. Still other seed fell on good soil. It came up and yielded a crop, a hundred times more than was sown."

"This is the meaning of the parable: The seed is the word of God. Those along the path are the ones who hear, and then the devil comes and takes away the word from their hearts, so that they may not believe and be saved. Those on the rock are the ones who receive the word with joy when they hear it, but they have no root. They believe for a while, but in the time of testing they fall away. The seed that fell among thorns stands for those who hear, but as they go on their way they are choked by life's worries, riches and pleasures, and they do not mature. But the seed on good soil stands for those with a noble and good heart, who hear the word, retain it, and by persevering produce a crop."

—Luke 8:5-8, 11-15

Chapter 1: Seeds of Encouragement

"Therefore encourage one another and build each other up, just as in fact you are doing."

—1 Thessalonians 5:11

——You are a miracle, not a mistake.

—*What are you looking at?*

The question is, what are you looking at? Yes, when you look at your reflection in the mirror, what is it that you're looking at? Do you answer the question in a positive manner or a negative one? Examples of positive thoughts would be, *I am beautiful, fearfully and wonderfully made.* Or is it, *I am pretty BUT I wish my thighs, ankles, legs, bust line, or buttocks were bigger?* What are we telling ourselves to suggest how we and others view our outer appearance? Well, envision what God says about our outer appearance. When you're tempted to look at yourself any other way than how God see's you, reflect on his creation and remember that God does not see you as man does. That's all that matters when it's all said and done.

"But the LORD said to Samuel, "Do not consider his appearance or his height, for I have rejected him. The LORD does not look at the things people look at. People look at the outward appearance, but the LORD looks at the heart."

—*1 Samuel 16:7 (NIV)*

—*"Life is a collection of divine and appointed moments."*

From this day forth, if change is what you seek, which opportunities and strategic appointments will you seek? Those that build you up, or those that tear you down? Yes, we have the ability to self-sabotage the divine connections, appointments, and opportunities that God would want for us, but our perspective is the key on which our goals hinge. When you're looking at that glass of milk, is it half full or is it half empty? Every bit of your answer is the course of life you have or will have. Search yourself to see which it is, half full or half empty.

—"Be in the environment you want to be in, NOT the one you have to be in."

When you aren't intentional about your destiny, environment, financial affairs, efforts, and your ultimate journey in life, you tend to loss control and default to undesired situations. Be in the environment you want as opposed to defaulting to those environments you don't want. That could be a less desirable relationship, place you live, work environment, career track, or, perhaps, educational program. The moral to the story is to be intentional about the environment you're in, which will enhance your overall quality of life. Yes, we have to desire a quality of life to attain that quality of life.

—*"Put your oxygen mask on first."*

In other words, how can we save another when we don't save ourselves first? Self-care is not only important, but vital. Yes, we have laundry to do, groceries to pick up, and homework to do with the kids, cooking and cleaning, and oh, how could I forget about work? *However,* if we don't take care of self, self won't take care of us. In putting your oxygen mask on first, you're being diligent about celebrating yourself, doing things to remind yourself that you are on your own to-do list, and everything you *need* and *have* to do will get done one step at a time. Without you in good health, mind, body, soul, and spirit, none of this is possible.

Quick visual: you are in the hospital suffering with anxiety and panic attacks so detrimental that you are in need of pure oxygen to breath. Not such a pretty sight is it? I know, been there, done that and the list continues no matter what, so put yourself at the top of the list. The rest will be done one step at a time.

—"Being fit is the new it."

Now that you've read this, what stands out that needs to change as far as putting everything before yourself? Write some things down and challenge yourself to change the course of how you view *self-care* or looking at yourself as a priority amidst everything else that *has* to be done per you. What are some things you intend to do to better take care of yourself?

Challenge to self:

_____

_____

_____

—*If not you, then who?*

If you aren't presenting yourself to the world every day, then who are you presenting? What I mean by that is, if you aren't being your authentic self, then who are you? If you are presenting one with non-original hair, nails, breast implants for cosmetic reasons only, buttocks, eyelashes, and other various parts of your body, then can we agree that isn't your original self? If you can't be yourself, then who is it that you are striving to be when you don't allow others to meet the real you? God made you very special and unique and the world is waiting to meet the real you. If you can't be inspired by your closest circle of associations, then you are in the wrong circle of associations. Hair, nails, eyelashes, Brazilian buttocks, breasts, etc. don't make the authentic you any better than God originally made you.

—Be a light in dark places.

We are to be the light of the earth. Many people are hurting, so when they cross your path, turn your light on and let it shine. You never know how keeping your light on can save a life. Your light could very well be a word of encouragement or support for another through a rough time. So turn your light on and let it shine brightly today and everyday as possible.

"You are the light of the earth. A city on a hill cannot be hidden. Neither do people light a lamp and put it under a bowl. Instead they put it on its stand, and it gives light to everyone in the house. In the same way, let your light shine before men, that they may see your good deeds and praise your Father in heaven."

—Matthew 5:14

—*"Back the train up to the station."*

In other words, back the train up to the station, and begin your route again. Are you in a disdainful relationship, or mindset? If so, back your train up to the station, refuel, and begin again. After all, the train must continue to keep moving throughout the tracks of life. The train keeps moving and waits for no one, occasionally stopping to refuel and let others on or off, but the train must continue.

Challenge to self: Notate who needs to get on or off your train. This is your route, your train, and ultimately your life. What needs to change for the direction of your life to pass through better stations, better options, or better choices?

_____

_____

_____

— *"You teach people how to treat you."*

If you show people it is okay to disrespect, belittle, and walk over your feelings in a distasteful manner, then you'll likely experience those disrespectful behaviors in return. Show them you are worthy, but know you're worthy first, so that your image doesn't suggest otherwise. When someone comes to you with foolish, distasteful, and disdainful treatment, your reaction makes the resounding difference. Is your reaction suggestive of how you see yourself? Mirror, mirror on the wall, who is the fairest of them all?

Challenge to self: write a note to yourself reminding you who in your circle is disrespectful to you, but you tolerate their behavior in the name of friendship, family status, or even love? No one is more valuable than your own self when it comes to treatment. See yourself as one who is worthy to be treated with respect, just as you respect others.

—*"Don't give anyone your power."*

If you have given much of your power to one who has not loved you properly and intends to take advantage of the pure love given to them freely from you, then it's time to take back your power. There's power in words, but also power in your silent actions. Either way, you'll get a reaction, but the goal is to get the right response. A response and reaction are two different things.

While there is so much power in what you say, there is more power in what you don't say. When people treat you disrespectfully, not saying anything and relinquishing them, as well as the situation, to God in your silence is more powerful than anything. I suggest not only praying about it, but eloquently standing your ground in a way in which a response is warranted, not giving that person the desired reaction. Yes, the devil will use anyone, and their mouth, to provoke you to act beneath your level.

We have to learn to have The Father speak to both your heart (as well as theirs) while you recover from the meekness and passivity caused when you're taken for granted. Simply put, don't go there with them any longer. Rather, keep your peace and keep your power. If you have to, keep it moving too! Life is simply too short to fight a *knit-picker's* battle.

——"Pick your battles, or stop fighting every battle that comes your way."

You can't fight a battle on the battlefield with a man that's at war within his own heart. It's a losing battle on the field, especially for you since the battle is in their minds and not in the physical realm, which isn't observable by another person. Trying to save someone who doesn't want to be saved is a losing battle. Your energy, effort, and excitement for life when the other wants to die is in vain; saving them may mean losing you. Rethink your strategy and begin again.

Have you ever heard the heroic story of the drowning victim that pulls the life guard down in distress and they both drown? This is the same idea.

Pick your battles wisely, and don't lower your standards to argue with a man on the battlefield of his heart. This is not your fight.

Challenge to self: who do you spend your time trying to right when they enjoy their wrongs? Whose savior are you? Explore and write out your exit strategy from battling them to winning within.

"Respond, don't react."

—*Unrealistic expectations + reality=*

Unrealistic expectations+ reality =disappointments & disasters. Set your mind on realistic expectations of others. We are all a work in progress. Allowing others to default to disappointment sets you up for reality and limits your liability of disappointments.

You can choose to use your power or choose to be powerless. Which choice will you exercise?

Challenge to self: what expectations currently exist within yourself that don't line up with reality?

—Divorce people's perspective.

You have to be you. In fact, be the best you that you can be. You are unique. You know your desires, tastes in life, and what is good for you. You're not above reproach from others, but walk out your life experiencing things for yourself. When people want to impress their lifestyle upon you, do your research to see if the lifestyle they may want to impose upon you is right for you. It could be that they want the best for you, and that's fine, but just be mindful that you have to make decisions based on what you can do. It could be that they want you to enlist yourself into a strict regimen such as drastically changing your eating habits, sleep habits or the way you worship. In the end YOU have to be satisfied with YOU.

How you live, how you worship, when you worship, where you worship, what you eat, or where you eat is meant to be enjoyable. You are not contained to "strict" religious principles. You have freedom in Christ. I salute you to find your freedom in Christ and enjoy the balance of life that God has given you through Christ. While people mean well, this is your life. If you follow people in their practices or strict regiments, you lose your balance in life, your true connection with God. Regiments of others may not suit you well at all.

God is fun, balanced, and loving, and he wants you to have freedom. Divorce humans and get your freedom back from human perspectives and opinions. Are you in captivity? Let yourself be free from what others think you should be, do, and enjoy in your life. It is a bi-lateral decision between you and God. Enjoy!

"See to it that no one takes you captive through hollow and deceptive philosophy, which depends on human tradition and the basic principles of this world rather than on Christ."

—Colossians 2:8

> *—"Check yourself before you wreck yourself."*

Self- evaluation is paramount. If not you, then who has the ability to check you when you're wrong, out of line, or acting in a distorted manner? We have to have the talk with the man in the mirror to learn more about ourselves and what God would want to do in our lives.

> —It's easier to fix you before you can fix another, which is impossible.

—*"Don't complain, comply."*

—Camille

Complaining enhances your problem to you, and it takes root to further harm if you're not careful. Complying with the necessary task gives God an opportunity to change the situation for you. Complaining means you remain where you are. Change your outcast by complying rather than complaining.

—You have a right to protect your peace.

It's your right to protect your peace because no one else will. When you come into any situation, whether a friendship or relationship, and you have had a peaceful life prior to your newfound relationship, you are required to maintain your level of peace. If not, you are susceptible to allowing others to alter, disconnect, and otherwise disengage your peace. Be a peace keeper, but first be a peace maintainer for you.

"Peace I leave with you; my peace I give you. I do not give to you as the world gives. Do not let your hearts be troubled and do not be afraid."

—John 14:27

— *"When you're peaceful, you're powerful."*

—*J. M.*

Walk in peace with the knowledge you gain in this life.

"The Lord will bless his people with peace."

—*Psalm 29:11*

—Manage your emotions, or your emotions will manage you.

"My dear brothers, take note of this: Everyone should be quick to listen, slow to speak and slow to become angry, for man's anger does not bring about the righteous life that God desires."

—James 1:19-20

When you get mad, as we are conditioned to do as human beings, you have a choice in what you choose to do with that emotion. You can either show the anger outwardly or show maturity by managing your emotions within. Regardless of the route you opt to take, what's inside of you will come out. We are destined to express ourselves one way or another. Which will it be for you? Will you manage your emotions or will your emotions manage you?

—If you don't handle the handle, the handle will handle you!

This can be applied to many areas of your life such as handling your business or whatever. In other words, handle your affairs, career choices, your love interest, your time, money, investments, purpose in life, your salvation, etc. We are to be aware of the conscious choices we make in life. Either we live life by default, or we live it by design and that means handling what we can handle. These are necessary things that we encounter daily that we have to handle, whether we want to or not. Otherwise we will allow the handle to handle us, and that can tend to default to a life that's uncontrolled.

"And let us not be weary in well doing: for in due season we shall reap, if we faint not."

—Galatians 6:9

—Its quitting time.

Quitting ahead of calamity is not the same as quitting. It takes wisdom to see the storm ahead and go in a different direction.

When you see the forecast, plan your course, but plan to include God's divine direction.

—Storms are designed to pass, not last.

A hurricane, tornado, mud slide, tsunami or something as simple as a rain storm is designed to last momentarily, not a lifetime. The common theme when any or all of these types of storms occur is the beautiful sunshine that tends to come out shortly after the storm has passed. The same can be applied to a storm that you may experience in life such as a layoff, divorce, health issue, financial turmoil, children issues, and all of the storms of life we face in this human lifetime. The question is, what perspective will you take while you're bunkered down as if you're in a hurricane, tornado or rain storm? Just as preparation to stay safe is a necessity while waiting for the storm to pass, the same applies for your personal storms to come and pass too. While your storms are passing through as we all face them, prepare with The Word, luxuriate in God's presence, and engulf yourself around positive people to help you pass through.

We are either preparing for a storm, in a storm, or just coming out of a storm. No one is exempt; the difference is the preparation, perspective and your ability to hold strong in God while it passes. After all, the sunshine is coming again soon.

—*The Eye of the Storm*

The eye of the perfect storm is noted as being "a period of time during a *storm* when things are calm." However, this doesn't mean that the storm is over. Things just get worse as the eye moves to the tail-end of the storm. Just as with any storm, prepare ahead of time, especially since we know that storms are inevitable, yet purposeful.

—*See the Rainbow*

We all want to see the rainbow after the storm but the rain has to come first. Yes, the rain represents your storm. Rainbows are beautiful and not often in plain view. However, they are breathtaking and worth the view when seen. Look, stare, and thank God that the storm is over, as represented by the rainbow.

—*You are not alone*

When you are facing adversity, challenges, and trials that seem to take the wind out of you, you are not alone. I know it may seem as if you're in the "*fight of your life*" but remember that you are not alone. How do I know this? It's Biblical, not an opinion. Challenges, problems, issues and adversity in this lifetime are inevitable; it's a matter of knowing that God himself is with you and will never leave you.

> "Do not fear, for I am with you; Do not anxiously look about you, for I am your God. I will strengthen you, surely I will help you, surely I will uphold you with my righteous right hand."
>
> —*Isaiah 41:10*

—*We forgive, but we don't forget.*

Everyone has been hurt or offended by someone in life. An essential that is a must for living a productive and hindrance-free life: forgive but don't forget. I say that because we are called to forgive, the forgetting isn't an automatic thing that happens for people. Realistically, forgetting should not be the case, so you can remember the experience enough to guard your heart from future transgressions and not be naïve to someone who may be preying on what they think is a weakness within you. Let's be honest, all intentions of others are not the purest towards those who are nice, sweet, good, and honorable; the nicest people are often easy targets to get dishonored, used, manipulated, and right out trampled upon from those who prey on light-hearted people.

Guard your heart and turn up your discernment, but forgive those who transgress, harm, hinder and hurt you. It's Biblical that we forgive, but we don't forget. Wish the manipulator well, forgive them even, but again, don't forget. Life tends to repeat itself like history, so there should be no surprise in seeing the manipulation again if you're not careful. Forgiving and forgetting are separate entities.

Five Stages to Help You Forgive

Share your story

Feel your feelings

Get the facts from your story

Visualize your story from a spiritual perspective

Use a healthy exercise to enhance healing

Share Your Story

In confidence, share your story with a trusted source, (i.e.) diary, friend, or relative. In detail, explore what happened that lead you to a place of feeling hurt, hindered, or injured. Tell your story with all details, so that you will get out what you're feeling for good.

Feel Your Feelings

Don't be afraid of what you feel. Feel what you feel; don't inhibit your natural feelings from coming forth. If you're mad, be mad, if you're confused, pray to God for that to pass, but acknowledge whatever you feel so that you are moving through the process of forgiving without any hold-ups; feel it. Whether it is sadness, discomfort, or grief -- your feelings are your feelings. Control your actions though, no matter what you feel because feelings should not control us.

Get the facts from your story

There are three sides to every story. Your side, the other side, and the truth of what happened that lead to you feeling the way you do, inspiring a need to forgive someone. I'm no judge or authority to suggest otherwise, but I would encourage you to see the other side of the story and gather the facts of what happened, with an emphasis on removing your emotions when you do. This may or may not be possible depending on timing, but try. Forgiveness is a must for you to move on.

Visualize your story from a spiritual perspective

Read the Bible in terms of what God says about your situation, forgiveness, the act of transgressions, peace, and humility for others. God's perspective is the best measure for forgiveness. It's Biblical that we walk in forgiveness even when humanly impossible.

Use a healing exercise to usher in forgiveness

Sometimes we need to find a way to make ourselves feel better and therefore let things go with others who have hurt, hindered, harmed, or used us. God is the best vindicator, and simply giving the situation to God to work out while we forgive is the best thing to do. At any rate, find a healing exercise that will entice you to lay the burden down and rest in God while forgiveness consumes your heart, mind, and emotions.

The following are light suggestions:

Pray

Sleep if off (rest)

Exercise (exhale)

Laugh (see a comedy show or movie)

Spend quality time with like-minded associates

Relax while reading your favorite book

Retreat (go away a few days)

Sabbatical from the world

Chapter 2:

Seeds for Love & Relationships

"Love is patient, love is kind. It does not envy, it does not boast, it is not proud. It is not rude, it is not self-seeking, it is not easily angered, and it keeps no record of wrongs. Love does not delight in evil but rejoices with the truth. It always protects, always trusts, always hopes, and always perseveres. Love never fails."

—1 Corinthians 13:4-8

—*A Living Sacrifice*

Don't live by the pressures of life, rather, live by priorities. What are your priorities? Give power to your priorities.

"Therefore, I urge you, brothers and sisters, in view of God's mercy, to offer your bodies as a living sacrifice, holy and pleasing to God—this is your true and proper worship."

—Romans 12:1 (NIV)

—*Baggage*

Have you ever considered the more we live, the more luggage we tend to pick up as we mature through life? Yes, we all have baggage or luggage that we carry around whether we believe it or not. The question is, are you willing to carry yours with another as no one human is perfect. Another question is, have you examined what type of baggage you carry? Yes, just as the TSA inspectors examine your luggage, you too have to examine, evaluate, and acknowledge that you carry luggage as you've traveled in life. The right person will welcome the idea of you unpacking your bags right before their eyes and oftentimes will help you with carrying your baggage too.

—*Irreplaceable*

You simply cannot replace what's not missed. When you're good to someone, you are simply irreplaceable. When someone is good to you beyond normal measures, the same applies. However, some are distorted in their view while taking you for granted, and think that another like you exists. Not so. You're simply irreplaceable.

—"When it fits, it simply fits."

You always know what it isn't even when you don't quite know what it is. You know what it is like trying on the perfect dress or suit? When you try it on, it simply fits, and you get that alluring feeling like "yes, this is it!" Second-guessing yourself in love is essentially settling for something that is not quite for you. No matter how you may adjust the relationship, if it isn't working, it's really simple; it isn't working.

When they want you, they will. In love and relationships there should not be any guessing games as to where you stand with one another. If so, you're not in a relationship. Count your losses and move on. You'll thank yourself later when you find the one or perhaps the one finds you.

— "*I can show you better than I can tell you.*"

Look at what the person *does*, not as much what is *said* when you hear the words *I love you*. I know it's easy for people to say "I love you," but showing you that they love you is just as good, if not for some who need to see it, better. When real love is present, not the *illusion of love*, it's easy to treat the loved one with dignity rather than disrespect and disdain. Ponder on some of the attributes of God's profound definition of what love is: patient, kind, hoping, not rude, not boastful, not easily angered, not self-seeking, and keeps no record of wrongs; love never fails. Anything other than God's supreme description of love is an *illusion* and non-truth.

So when that person says, "I love you," are you seeing these attributes of love, per God?

Challenge to self: if in a relationship, write about the type of love you are you giving and receiving. Assess the situation. If your version of love isn't Biblical, it's an *illusion*.

God gives the perfect definition, man may disagree with that, but that's okay. God's word is truth.

_____

_____

_____

> *—"If the shoe doesn't fit, don't force it on."*

Wear the right shoe size (relationship) that fits, otherwise, you're destined to get a sore toe, bunion, or the like. While this is a metaphor, the same applies to being in the wrong relationships that we force to fit in our lives. All of it is painful either way.

The same can be stated for the perfect gloves that may be too tight. When it's not the right size, it simply will not fit. You have a well-fitted shoe (person) waiting for your cozy feet as well as your hands that need warming. Wait for the right size unless you want to be uncomfortable with someone else's shoe size or perhaps glove size. If it's not working, take that wrong size off for relief.

> *— "If it doesn't fit, you must acquit."*
>
> *—Attorney Johnny Cochran*

—He saved the "best" for last.

Believe and know this: if it's a relationship you're wanting, and you're surveying all the mistakes you've made, know that there is still time for God to help you fulfill his plans and will for your life. He truly has saved the best for last. If you're not living your best life, this is a clear indication that it's not over. God is up to something because he's saving the best for last, even for you in love and your ultimate relationship that you are waiting for.

—Jeremiah 29:11

—*Front window or the rear- view mirror?*

Are you looking out of the front windshield or the rear-view mirror when you drive your vehicle? What if you had to drive your car while only viewing your rear-view mirror? Surely, many car accidents would be inevitable if this were the case. It's almost the same metaphor when you constantly look back, reach back, entertain, and not *fully* disconnect, discard, or dissipate the feelings from the past with an *ex*-partner, spouse, or inappropriate connection. In essence, that's what you'll opt to do when you drive looking in the rear-view mirror, which is only intended to be a quick glance, instead of trusting God by looking through the large front window.

You **cannot** have God's best in your **next** if you constantly entertain the rear view mirror (**ex**). You're destined to crash your car each time. Look forward in front-view mode, so that you can reach your **best** instead of gripping the hand of your **ex**, which is an **ex** for a reason.

—*"The power of agreement."*

"Do two walk together unless they have agreed to do so?"

—Amos 3:3

Are you praying, praising, and joyfully playing with your significant other? My guess is that we should be able to do all three. Otherwise, what's the point of having a significant other? By definition, a significant other is one with whom you can share life's ups, downs, treasures, excitements, praise reports, pitfalls, and top experiences with. Who would pair with one who cares less for your desirables? Many do, hence the need to survey this ahead of time before you make the dreadful mistake of not choosing a like-minded mate.

——Before agreeing with another I must first agree with me, myself, and I that the one I seek agreement from is in fact the "one".

—*Are you reasoning with insanity?*

The definition of insanity is expecting different results *although* you've done the same things.

Yes, by definition insanity is expecting a different result by doing the same things. Are you entertaining someone that oftentimes argues with you about trivial matters that make no sense? Be done with trying to "reason" with insanity; be done with explanations, arguments, and anything/anyone not of like mind; have some fun, have some peace, and live your life to the fullest. Kindly excuse those trying to interrupt this. You have a lot to live for and the best to look forward to.

Challenge to self: Write down who you need to stop arguing with, trying to convince you're a gift as a significant other, friend, or simply someone who loves to "push your buttons" in a negative way. You know who they are, so be honest.

_____

_____

—*Mission of life*

Who is your mate and what is your mission? These are two worthy things to ponder when thinking about your spouse. The answer to each, your mate and your mission, very well could change the course of your life.

—"Let your yes be yes and no be no."

Consider your thoughts when it comes to making a lifetime commitment or decision prior to that of the other one. You have to be true to yourself first before you can be true to another person. When you get to a certain point in life, cut the fluff and let your *yes* be what it is --*yes*. The same goes for your *no*'s, especially if you know that person is not the one for you. When you drag things on, you delay the inevitable because you don't want to ruffle their day; it's confusing to the one you're communicating with. Besides that, the Evil One is present because evil is truly the author of confusion. God has you and this profound scripture in mind when considering whether this is the person for you or not. It's not me, but God who wanted us to know that we have to be firm in our decisions. We don't need to embellish our decisions, stand firm on them. God has your back.

> "Simply let your Yes be yes and you're No, No; anything beyond this comes from the evil one."
>
> *—Matthew 5:37*

—What is the meaning of a relationship?

You won't destroy a relationship if you understand its purpose. When you know this is the person you'll never want to be without, you tend to treat the person with white gloves. You love them enough to be intentional. Otherwise, let's be honest with one another, you'll tend to mistreat, disrespect, and ultimately not care enough about the person if he or she is **not** "the one."

—"Marriage is a gift and covenant with God."

It's purposeful, and it's God. The world does give us options, but that doesn't mean the world is a buffet and we sample everything. Only when you're struggling with supreme truth will you take this approach by experiencing other things outside of this succinct covenant. When you know God's intentional plan for marriage, you will honor the sanctity, unity, freedom, and the ministry of marriage.

—"*Seal the cracks in your relationship.*"

It is a common practice to have to seal cracks in various structures. Sometimes using sealants is a necessity, so what needs to remain intact will stay that way. Sealant, in a sense, is like the necessary glue to hold things in place and seal up holes so what needs to stay out will stay out and what needs to stay in will stay in. Are you unhappy in your relationship? If that's the case, put some sealant in your relationship by doing things that add value to it and strengthen it. Here are some suggestions: pray together, worship together, play together, work out together, eat at the dinner table together, etc.

When you had unwanted things creep into your relationship, such as the other woman or man, you left your crack untreated, and didn't fill it with sealant! Occasionally, sealant is a necessity to keep what needs to remain and keep out what should not be welcomed.

—"Control-Alt-Delete."

We can learn a lot from a computer especially when the screen tends to freeze up while we're in the middle of working on something important. It's no secret how to get a reset; it's oftentimes necessary to press *control-alt-delete* to get the computer to restart or unfreeze. If you're blessed, you may be able to recapture the work you were working on prior to the technological issue, but frequently it's a complete loss.

Along the route of life, specifically in relationships, it's a good idea to proactively *control-alt-delete.*

Control the situation: emotionally, mentally and physically.

*Alt*ernate your views so that you'll be open for God to bless you miraculously in the relationship provided that you're equally yoked.

Delete (as necessary) the debris in your life whether it be toxic relationships(male and female), mindsets, habitual sin habits, and anything that will hinder you in mind, body, soul, or spirit.

Like plants that need to be pruned to grow, we must learn to prune as we grow and that involves a routine of *control-alt-delete*.

—*Power of unity*

Have you ever wondered why the unity candle at weddings is lit in the presence of the minister, couple, and witnesses? It goes back to the power of unity with The Three; the couple in agreement with The Trinity in the perspective of those who can see beyond just the simplistic idea of candles uniting two people. Take an alternative perspective in seeing the two lives joining in agreement to becoming one with The Trinity; *God*, the *Son* and *Holy Spirit*.

"Again, I tell you that if two of you on earth agree about anything you ask for, it will be done for you by my father in heaven. For where two or three come together in my name, there am I with them."

——*Matthew 18:19*

—*Two is better than one*

We were not meant to live a life alone. God's word does not lie. Who can argue that two is better than one? A table for one is not as fun as table for two, so you can share your daily agenda, your plans, excitements, and ultimately, your life with another. Life is destined for two rather than one; don't believe the lie that God has placed you here to live life alone. Whether you pair with another friend, partner, or lifetime spouse, life is worth sharing with another because two really is better than one. However, be intentional on "table for two" being an equal partnership.

"Two are better than one; because they have a good reward for their labor."

——*Ecclesiastes 4:9-12 (KJV)*

An exit doesn't need an introduction. When it's over in love relationships, it's simply over.

—*Rejection & Redirection*

Man's rejection can be looked upon as God's protection or perhaps re-direction. No one likes rejection, but it's inevitable in life. The difference is how we look at being rejected. For some, it's "woe is me," for others it could be, "wonderful now I'm free to do and be me." The choice is yours but understand that when you're rejected, it's not about you. Simply put, don't beat yourself up because the person handing down the rejection just might be protecting you from something ahead in which you don't need to be apart. Accept rejection and understand its two-fold: God's protection and re-direction.

Chapter 3: Seeds for Friendships

"A man of many companions may come to ruin, but there is a friend who sticks closer than a brother."

—Proverbs 18:24

"Real friends want you to have the best and not negate to less."

"The wrong people will always do wrong to the right people."

"The right people will always be done wrong by the wrong people."

"The right people will always treat the wrong people right."

"Good friends are like stars. You don't always see them, but you know they are always there."

—*"If you run with wolves, you will learn how to howl. But if you associate with eagles, you will learn how to soar to great heights."*

—*anonymous*

Tell me who your best friends are, and I will tell you who you are. Have you surveyed the growth of your friends and closest associates? Have you taken the time to seek strength within your friendships that are designed to help propel you further in life? If you are the strength in your circle of your associates and can never get strength from those you associate with, then you may have outgrown your circle or perhaps need to be in a better circle. Just as food expires, so do friendships when they've reached their limitations and are no longer conducive to where you are in life or desire to be.

—Who are you REAL friends?

Do not waste your time, money, and energy on people that will not take you places. Life is about growing in positive directions. Where are you going, or where are the people you spend your time with taking you? In life, re-evaluating friendships as time passes is a healthy thing if you are not seeing the fruits of your friendships helping you grow to become the best person you can become. Do you need to re-evaluate? Search your thoughts, so that you can grow, unless you're interested in remaining at the same place and stage in your life.

"God has the ability to open the right doors and close the wrong doors."

> *—Who in your inner circle has you UP, DOWN or STUCK?*
>
> —*wise men*

In business, life, and even your ministry, you always need to assess and self- evaluate **who** or **what** helps your business grow **up**, get **stuck**, or sink **down**. Take a look within your relationships, partnerships, ventures and even your inner circle. You might just be surprised. If you don't take a look, it just might cost you more time, effort, and energy.

—*Tree People*

The Leaves: seasonal friends, fair weatherers that will wither away when their season is up like leaves falling from a tree.

Branches: people who are an extension of you. Their season in your life is much stronger and longer.

Roots: people that hold you up to help you live a strong and healthy life. They are grounded and a friend for life oftentimes.

The difference with where I am and where I'd like to be usually is one person. Who is in your tree?

Question: who are your leaves, branches and roots?

—*Your favorite five*

Show me who your friends are, and I'll tell you who you are. Associations will determine your altitude just like your attitude in life. Choose both wisely, that is your friends/associations as well as your attitude. Have you surveyed your association list lately? Have you surveyed the altitude in life you'd like to reach? Surveying both is worth ten minutes of your time. Seeking God for divine revelation and direction with associations and friendships can charter the course of your life if you're not careful. Pondering this could prove to be highly beneficial.

Associations either bring out the best in you or the worst in you. Either good intentions or the reverse are coming your way when you are considering your associations.

> "Do not be misled: Bad company corrupts good character."
>
> —*1 Corinthians 15:33*

—Iron sharpens Iron

Friends want you better, not bitter. They want you sharpened and the best in life. Friends want you to be the **best** *you* that you were designed to be. Those who suggest otherwise are **haters**, envious and jealous people. Don't fool yourself into thinking that those who are appearing close are only close to contribute to you becoming great. The alternative is that the observer has no intent of making you better. *Haters* are just there to be nosey or enjoy your resources and whatever else they stand to benefit from you while in your life. Believe it or not, Haters and envious people want a front row view into your life, so they don't miss a thing!

Let's take the time to thank the *real* people that contribute to our greatness today and every day. We are all connected to one another and by far not designed to become great alone! We need one another, so be selective about who you choose as being on your *way to greatness* team.

"As iron sharpens iron, so one man sharpens another."
——*Proverbs 27:17*

Haterade vs. Gatorade

Your candle doesn't burn brighter by blowing out the next person's candle. If you know something that would help your friend, relative, or associate excel in life, don't be an information hoarder, help them succeed. This approach has the ability to be just as refreshing as a glass of *Gatorade*. Both your candles can shine brightly unless you're what we call a *hater*.

—*Has your well run dry?*

Do you know that every well needs replenishing sometimes? You have to wonder where the water comes from and truly understand everyone needs replenishing when your water fountain, your brook, or well runs dry. The question is, after you've poured out all of your water from either place, do you have the right type of people covering you to help replenish you? If not, you're simply entertaining takers and not givers. There is a difference.

—"Winning is contagious, so is losing."

What are the dynamics of your team? Everyone either plays to win or they play to lose, whether or not it's realized or confessed. Subconsciously, your team could be either helping you win the game of life or perhaps inspiring your losses. Take a good look at your team. Team members are comprised of family, friends, acquaintances, associates, etc.

—*Your water fountain*

When we walk up to a water fountain, although they are few and far between these days, we still expect water when we push the button. The last thing one expects is for the water fountain to be out of service or perhaps out of water. The water fountain represents you if your circle of people constantly drinks from your water fountain but never replenishes you. You give, give, and give, and they never give back to you.

You are constantly pouring refreshing water into them but you often come up dry. Re-evaluate your circle so that you too can be replenished when the well providing water runs dry.

Chapter 4: Seeds of Inspiration

"If it is encouraging, let him encourage; if it is contributing to the needs of others, let him give generously; if it is leadership, let him govern diligently; if it is showing mercy, let him do it cheerfully."

—Romans 12:8

—Let go of the mess in exchange for God's best.

Question: what would change in the world if you simply changed your mind? Change your mind and be intentional about pursuing your purpose, calling and your earth's assignment!

"And there were four leprous men at the entering in of the gate: and they said one to another, Why sit here until we die?"

—*2 Kings 7:3 (KJV)*

—I changed my mind. I hope you will too.

—I'm not where I want to be.

You're not where you used to be either. Thank God he delivered you from where you used to be although you're not where you want to be. In this case, you have many thanks since yes God delivered you from where you were to here. You can continue to travel where you'd like to be, but without him, this isn't possible.

"I can do all things through Christ who strengthens me."

—Philippians 4:13

Confess with me: I thank God for delivering me from where I used to be.

Celebrate your future& thank God for deliverance from your past.

—Doing what God wants

"Now when he had left speaking, he said unto Simon, Launch out into the deep, and let down your nets for a draught. And Simon answering said unto him, Master, we have toiled all the night, and have taken nothing: nevertheless at thy word I will let down the net. And when they had this done, they enclosed a great multitude of fishes: and their net brake."

—Luke 5:4-6 (KJV)

Jesus as he was in the boat with other disciples suggested that they "launch into the deep." In fact, not only was it a suggestion, it was actually a directive so that they would change the course of the results of their labor. Sometimes we have to launch into the deep with what God wants for our lives and not living by default of what we think we should be doing. This passage is paramount because the disciples were like average people; they toiled with different occupations but at the end of the day, their obedience to the Lord's words prospered all of their efforts. In essence, we should follow suit and do what sayeth the Lord.

Launch Into the Deep!

—"*If you want nothing, you have nothing to do.*"

If you want nothing out of this journey of life and merely exist day to day, then you have nothing to do to improve your current circumstances. If you're in tune with the fact that God gave you a divine purpose in life, an assignment to fulfill while on this earth then this is for you. You have to fight for your missions, your goals, and your calling in life to become a reality. Nothing just happens; people first decide to make things happen, or they watch as things happen. Those that make things happen are coupled with faith in God and his perfect timing.

However, don't negate the fact that you have some things to do. I don't prescribe a peachy experience or a perfect journey, but I can guarantee that God is on this route and journey with you.

Your assignment holds the keys to your *peace, passion* and, ultimately, your *prosperity.* Go for it!

—"Because you're not there yet doesn't mean you're not going."

Keep going and don't stop until you reach your targeted destination. If you're not where you want to be, then you still have to keep going. Keep pushing, believing, persevering, and striving. Greatness is just up ahead on the right, but you won't get there if you stop where you are.

"You whom I have taken from the ends of the earth, And called from its remotest parts And said to you, 'You are My servant, I have chosen you and not rejected you."

—Isaiah 41:9

—— *"Until you're committed nothing will happen; once you're committed everything will happen."*

When you have a goal in mind to reach, you have to commit to reaching your goal. Goals could include changing your diet habits, wardrobe, level of education, career path or relationship appropriateness. You won't commit to what you're not committed to.

——Winners win, losers lose.

—*Three prominent enemies: could have, should have, & would have.*

Three enemies: could'a, should'a, & would'a tend to have the power to take your joy out of the day. Could have, should have, and would have are joy breakers because they indicate the need to look back with regrets. To reflect backwards on these three doesn't promise to help *anything*! However, on the positive, you can use these three as strategies for charting better options, choices, and ultimately a better perspective. Today is a new day.

Challenge to self: write what you could have, should have or would have done differently that will warrant the results you desire. Convert these three from enemies to powerful thoughts that will propel you higher in life.

_____

_____

_____

—"If you aim at nothing, you will hit it every time."

"Write down the revelation and make it plain on tablets so that a herald may run with it."

—Habakkuk 2:2

Life is about purpose. Having a vision can help that. When God shows you a vision of things to come or confirms your purpose in life, it's paramount to take heed and write down the ideas that are deposited to you. If you explore, meditate on what God has shown you or the ideas that he's calling you to implement into action, life is simple. God meant his revelation and vision to be made plain, not hidden for loss. Those desires you have for more, those business ideas, books, education you desire to study, career you admire -- are all heaven-sent. What you do with the gift of revelation and vision is up to. It could make the difference of a life fulfilled or one less desired.

Challenge to self: what has God shown you to do that you need to write down? Goals written tend to come to pass.

—"It's not always your fight; pick your battles wisely."

You may be on the battlefield, but you may not be there to fight. Suppose you're there for training and to learn how to fight by observation. Every battle isn't yours to fight; some things are meant only as lessons to learn and prepare you for your own fight when the time comes because we all face battles. In the meantime, pick your battles wisely, so productivity in other areas of life that matter isn't lost.

— "Tough times don't always last but tough people do."

—"Good thoughts versus bad thoughts."

If you don't talk to yourself (good thoughts), yourself will talk to you (bad thoughts)...what are you saying to yourself today? Sometimes the mind will play tricks on you. It's a human thing (not always the right thing), but it can happen in this lifetime. Your thoughts turn into choices, deeds, and actions. Feed your thoughts with positive outcomes or your life will head in the opposite direction. What are your thoughts saying to you?

"Finally, brothers and sisters, whatever is true, whatever is noble, whatever is right, whatever is pure, whatever is lovely, whatever is admirable--if anything is excellent or praiseworthy--think about such things."

——*Philippians 4:8*

——*"What you think about, you bring about."*

——*wise men*

—A. N. T. S.

Automatic **N**egative **T**houghts -- get rid of them. Just like fire ants hurt when they bite, so does an **A**utomatic **N**egative **T**hought. Get some ant eaters: good thoughts, good friends, and positive people around you to kill those ANTS!

"For my thoughts are not your thoughts, neither are your ways my ways, declares the Lord."

—*Isaiah 55:8*

Our actions are given directions with our thoughts. Which direction are your thoughts taking you today?

—Crazy thoughts

Crazy thoughts don't make you crazy, only when you believe them. Not only is it crazy to believe crazy thoughts, but crazier when they are acted out.

—*What do you want?*

To get what you never had, do what you've never done. Challenge yourself today to do what you have never done to get what you've never had. Otherwise, you should expect the same results if you do the same thing. Do you want something for nothing? That's what we call insane, doing the same thing and expecting a different result.

—— Be different to get different results.

—— Nothing will change until you change how you see and pursue the difference you desire.

—— You can't change the past but you can hit the reset button to form a plan of action to change your future.

"Fear thou not; for I am with thee: be not dismayed; for I am thy God: I will strengthen thee; yea, I will help thee; yea, I will uphold thee with the right hand of my righteousness."

——*Isaiah 41:10 (KJV)*

—When you know what you want, what you don't want becomes much clearer.

Have you ever considered that what you don't want in life has been what you've gravitated towards routinely? It's no wonder the same results have manifested. Oftentimes, our instincts tell us that this mate, education track, house, job, or career path isn't for us. But what do we do? We continue down a road out of habit, routine, someone else's choice for us and many other ideas that lend themselves to us settling. As you grow and mature in life, what you want becomes much clearer because you would have counted up the many occasions that you didn't have what you wanted. Go for it regardless and start where you are. Where you are isn't where you'll finish. If you don't start, then yeah, you've decided that you're finished.

—Productivity has a purpose; "we can pay now or pay later."

I like the idea of retirement, so paying now sounds better. I don't want to pay later by working until the day I leave this earth especially if it is at a less desirable place. Tap into your purpose today.

Are you playing or paying today? If you spend more time playing when it should be paying in five years what will life look like? Life is a balance, pay some, play some, but pay more attention to that which you'd rather do more often in your later years.

A quick visual: you're working at a fast food restaurant in your later years with children young enough to be your great grand-children. Paying now really isn't such a bad option in that context.

Note to self: No pain, no gain. Paying can be painful, but gaining (playing) is wonderful!

—24 hours a day

What dreams have been placed on your heart to complete? Recognize that within a day, you have time to cultivate your purpose and the dreams planted within you to fulfill. They may be small, or they may be large but be lead and follow through so that your prosperity can arrive. Don't put off something to complete tomorrow that needs to be completed today.

You are a solution provider just as someone else is your solution. Connect with your solution provider as well as producing your solution to the earth today. You have a healthy assignment and call on your life which encompasses your purpose to fulfill. Remember you're a solution provider. Be where your answer is, but release your answer to someone waiting for you too today!

"If we fail to prepare our day, we subconsciously prepare to fail in our day."

—"To have what others don't you have to do what others won't."

Are you in a circle of mediocrity? When you look at your situation, even if you're looking into your circle of influence such as family and friends, do your lifestyles look alike? To have what others don't, especially if they aren't walking in their full potential, you have to stay focused on doing the opposite of what you've seen if it hasn't been productive, successful, and fruitful. If you want more, do more. If you want better, do better.

——We are what we repeatedly do. If it's nothing, then that's pretty sure to deliver expected results: nothing.

—*"If you're tired of starting over, cease giving up! Focus on your purpose, pray about your plans and go forward with God as your Global Position System."*

If anything I know, God will never mislead you. If you have an ear to listen to his voice, he will order your steps, guide your path, and lead you right into greatness.

"In all your ways acknowledge him, and he will make your paths straight."

—*Proverbs 3:6*

—*"If you save money, money will save you."*

If you don't save money, money won't be there to save you. We need to stop buying what we *want*, and then *begging* for what we need. Do something different; *save*, *invest*, and *learn* to respect money so money will take care of *you*.

If you don't control your money, your money **will** *control you.* It will determine how and where you live. *What* and *if* you'll drive a vehicle. In what zip code your children will receive an education, where you'll work, and so forth. Money controls more than you think. Respect your wallet and pocket book, so a healthy collaboration is in order.

Are you a check away from being homeless? You can rearrange the sinking ship, but it's still going down if you don't seize the right mindset to respect your money.

—"Amazing people can do amazing things. You are amazing."

Every morning while it's early in the day you have time to set the tone for the day, so that the enemy doesn't set the tone for *your* day. He is *hired* daily by many to kill, steal, and destroy. He kills us by sending negative thoughts, somber distractions, ideas, people, and associations that take us away from God's good will and plans for our lives.

"The thief comes only to steal and kill and destroy; I have come that they may have life, and have it to the full."

——John 10:10

—"Take a licking, but keep it ticking."

May the beat go on. The beat of your heart that is what says you're still alive. As long as you're alive you can still overcome obstacles, challenges, and all the likes that suggest problems are near. We all must persevere through various issues. To have obstacles is normal. Again, you're alive; the ticking can outweigh the licking. No one likes being beat up with issues, problems, deception, or financial problems, but keep ticking to better days to come. You can do it!

—*You have a decision to make.*

Have you ever had a decision to make, and it troubled you so much that you struggled with the decision? Sleepless nights that seem to last so long because the decision is wavering on your mind? You wonder do you go left, or do you go right? Well, in God there is no confusion. He gives us peace, freedom, and liberty to make a sound decision and live with it. When it's God, it's good. When its evil, it's hard, confusing and resembles a counterfeit. Be careful the only real thing is the one who comforts and counsels, and that would not be the evil one.

Where your peace is, so is your answer.

"Peace I leave with you; my peace I give you. I do not give to you as the world gives. Do not let your hearts be troubled and do not be afraid."

—*John 14:27*

—*What is your purpose for living?*

"For I know the plans I have for you," declares the Lord, "plans to prosper you and not to harm you, plans to give you hope and a future."

—*Jeremiah 29:11*

Your purpose in life is directly correlated to your life assignment. Yes, we have all been called by God to fulfill something while living on this earth. You ever wonder why really successful people look radiant, healthy, and financially beaming like a radiant light? I am almost certain that they have pledged to work on their God-given assignment, purpose in life, and gifts. More often than not, they are happy because God's intent for man is to be happy while you are toiling and working on your life's mission. Your money is attached to your obedience in seeking and lining up with your purpose.

—You have an assignment.

Although we are not in school, a test still exists. God will prepare you, and preparation is not often an easy task to accept. You will be challenged while being prepared to walk out your purpose, but don't give up because your breakthrough and your blessings, including financial provisions, are attached to your assignment, which again includes a test. For some, it will be what feels like the test of life. God's intent is for you to prosper, so don't lose sight of that important thought.

Prepare and study; be mindful of your perspective, but be obedient. If you fail the test for your assignment, The Tester will re-test you. Until you pass the test, you will be tested while in preparation for your God-given talents to be sharpened, so that you can live a prosperous life.

It's Biblical, not an opinion.

—2 Timothy 2:15

The question is: how bad do you want your provisions, blessings, breakthroughs, and, ultimately, freedom in knowing you are walking out your life's mission?

Study, study and study more as the test of life will appear often.

—*Are you pregnant*?

"When Elizabeth heard Mary's greeting, the baby leaped in her womb, and Elizabeth was filled with the Holy Spirit."

—Luke 1:41

First, second, and third trimesters of gestation can be similar to that of different seasons and stages of life. When a woman is carrying an unborn child in the first stages of the pregnancy, she is subject to having morning sickness, and vomiting frequently during this stage. Formation of many vital organs is taking place and although you cannot see the physical manifestation of her baby, she still has evidence that she's expecting. The question is: what is growing inside of you like Mary that keeps leaping, but all the while makes you feel nauseated at times and encompasses all of the normal symptoms of pregnancy?

First trimester symptoms include morning sickness.

Second semester symptoms include routine cravings although this phase is more comfortable because of the notion that the baby (your purpose) is gaining momentum and growing.

Third semester symptoms include the uncomfortable feelings of the pressure as the baby continues to grow. You may experience a lack of sleep and the wavering weight will continue to be applied to you as your baby (purpose) grows. All of a sudden, your water breaks, and the real pushing begins. Protect your baby.

The final stages of pregnancy include getting in the birth canal, baring down, and going forward with the birth of the baby. God is capable of conception which is a miracle. You can either birth or terminate; the choice is yours.

While this describes the process of gestation, pregnancy, and expectation, this applies to you and that calling on your life; the business, the ministry, the career -- whatever associated with what God has called you to do. As long as you have an unborn baby inside of you, uncomfortable pressure, cravings, lack of sleep, and the aforementioned symptoms are bound to be present. God is calling you to birth your baby.

Know this. You are carriers of someone's solution and miracle. Your baby, like Jesus, is the miracle so powerful that we each carry a solution to someone's success. The same applies to you. If someone else doesn't go forward with the birthing of their baby (their purpose), then your dream can be impeded also. You get it. We are all apart and connected in some sort of way because the dream only works with teamwork. The illusion is to be trapped by the "me concept."

—Do what you can where you are.
——Wise men

You have a goal to meet, but you haven't begun to work on it. Do what you can right where you are. Write down your goals and daily take the time to cultivate what's in your heart. Whether it's to write a book, start a business, get healthier or married, work on it daily and you'll be surprised with your progress or completion. Where you are is a divine place because it is the beginning of greatness, but remember -- it is about perspective. Humble beginnings count just like grand beginnings, whether big or small, the goal is to begin.

A great couple:

Passion & Purpose

—"*Don't believe everything you hear.*"

What do I mean? I'm glad you asked. If you believe everything you hear without doing your own analysis or investigative studies, you may sway without having your own grounded convictions. If you stand for nothing, you'll fall for everything every time. Some things require your belief system to decide for you.

—"Life is not perfect, but it isn't terrible either."

"We learn as we go along in life. Remember we've never lived this life before so get better, not bitter."

—*Dr. Leroy Wright*

Sometimes we have to be content where we are until we grow where we'd like to be.

You can still advance in the midst of adversity.

——"You have to see the picture first to seize the big picture. Vision is powerful and not to be taken lightly."

Everyone has an imagination, dreams, and, believe it or not, visions from God above. The goal is to write those visions and dreams down when we see them. There's nothing wrong with imagining a better life, scenario, or situation to come. Imagination comes from images, which in turn are powerful pictures. Don't take them lightly but better yet, ask God to help you in making those dreams become your reality.

"Write down the revelation and make it plain on tablets so that a herald may run with it."

—Habakkuk 2:2

—Are you living your dream or in the middle of a nightmare?

Nothing is impossible for you.
God holds your world in his hands.

Jesus looked at them and said, "With man this is impossible, but with God all things are possible."

—Matthew 19:26 (NIV)

Chapter 5: Seeds for Salvation

"Those who hope in the Lord will renew their strength. They will soar on wings like eagles; they will run and not grow weary, they will walk and not faint."

—Isaiah 40:31

—Heaven is real, so is hell.

Where will you choose to spend your eternity?

"He will punish those who do not know God and do not obey the gospel of our Lord Jesus. They will be punished with everlasting destruction and shut out from the presence of the Lord and from the glory of his might."

—2 Thessalonians 1:8-9 (NIV)

"The way of life is above to the wise, that he may depart from hell beneath."

—Proverbs 15:24 (KJV)

—Be fruitful in life.

You can if you remain in him.

With God we can accomplish what he has called us to do if we remain in him. Taking the alternative route will be harder.

"I am the vine; you are the branches. If a man remains in me and I in him, he will bear much fruit; apart from me you can do nothing."

——John 15:5

—Repent and begin again.

"Remember the height from which you have fallen! Repent and do the things you did first. If you do not repent, I will come to you and remove your lampstand from its place."

—Revelations 2:5

—From sin to salvation

"All of us also lived among them at one time, gratifying the cravings of our sinful nature objects of wrath. But because of his great love for us, God who is rich in mercy, made us alive with Christ even when we were dead in transgressions —it is by grace you have been saved."

——Ephesians 2:3

—*Looking back but walking forward*

"And to put on the new self, created to be like God in true righteousness and holiness."

——Ephesians 4:24

There is no future in looking into your past. When you look backwards, you tend to focus on the problem instead of looking forward at the promises of God. Look forward and grow forward in Christ, not backwards, as best you can. God's word is full of promises because in this life he knew we would have problems.

Focus on the promise, not the problem.

—*Which team are you on?*

Satan initiates who he doesn't own. His initiations manifest in many forms: sin, distractions, unequally yoked associations, and deception. But his tactics to recruit those who he finds a threat to his team are sleek, slick, and slow, but they are surely aggressive in nature. Once he has successfully initiated you into the kingdom of darkness, the appearance is that life looks great, and he'll leave you alone. His primary purpose is to lure you away from your purpose and disguise his plan to deceive you. He's a manipulator. The question is, whose voice will you listen to? Yours, His or His? The difference in the "His" is whether you solicit God, or the Devil; both want to be your daddy. Who will be your father, or better stated: who's your daddy? We all have one.

Once Satan has you on his team, he no longer needs to entice you with drugs, alcohol, and fornication. All of the vices of the world that stunt your growth and ability to be a successful player for the eternal team are tactics of the enemy. If he has you, you are made to overcome. So repent and began again.

He doesn't recruit who he owns. If your life is perfect and all of your wishes come true, and you're not saved, check your salvation because we are joint heirs with Christ and his life was not perfect. He tempted Jesus too. He suffered before the cross (purpose), and so shall we. Don't be discouraged beyond normal human repair.

"Brothers, my heart's desire and prayer to God for the Israelites is that they may be saved."

—Romans 10:1

—*Directions to Heaven: turn right, keep straight.*

—*"Wise men"*

"I am the Lord your God, who teaches you what's best for you, who directs you in the way you should go."

—*Isaiah 48:17*

You can check Google maps, MapQuest or any other source besides the final Global Positioning System (God), but the Bible makes it clear on these directions: turn right and keep straight! Seek the right road and live your live as whole, not broken, with nothing missing or in pieces.

—*Which way are you going?*

We should only want to go in the direction God is leading us. However, when you get to a fork in the road, sometimes you need directions. Do you go left or right? The direction can ultimately determine the course of life, so choosing your direction wisely is key. Your GPS or navigation system may be off-balance, but God is your direction. Other directions lead to destruction and ultimately a dark path.

"For, the one who desires life, to love and see good days, must keep his tongue from evil and his lips from speaking deceit. He must turn away from evil and do good; he must seek peace and pursue it. For the eyes of the lord are toward the righteous, and his ears attend to their prayer, but the face of the lord is against those who do evil."

——*1 Peter 3:10-12*

—Life is a test, and you're in class.

Life is a test, and we are constantly in the classroom being tested. Yes, the test can be in the form of repeated strings of distractions, trials, tribulations, downward spirals, setbacks, and anything that has the appearance of a storm in your life. In life, you're in the classroom constantly learning lessons. The key is that you must study while you struggle in certain areas such as finances, being a parent (if single), a spouse in a difficult marriage, or perhaps waiting to be married to the love of your life.

Take notes and study them wisely with pure intention, so that when the test of life comes (and it will), you will have learned a valued lesson to progress you to the next stage of your life. We live life in seasons, so you're bound to see things repeat themselves if you're not careful. The alternative view is that you run the test three or four times to get the results you want.

If you flunk the course, you'll have to repeat it anyway.

—"*Extraordinary people do extraordinary things.*"

"But you are a chosen, a royal priesthood, a holy nation, a people belonging to God, that you may declare the praises of him who called you out of darkness into his wonderful light."

—1 Peter 2:9

Today, do what's right and not just what's easy. Help someone, be someone's miracle, solution, and most importantly, their blessing. You are capable of being all three: miracle, solution, and blessing. Choose to be *extraordinary*.

—*Run your own race*

If you run with the Lord, he will order your steps and pace your run while you seek him for daily direction. In the meantime, run *your* race, not that of another. In other words, stay in *your* lane.

"….and let us run with perseverance the race marked out for us."

—*Hebrews 12:1*

—*Pace yourself*

There's a difference between growing and swelling although things that swell seem as if they are growing. Slow growth is much better than a quick swelling; stay encouraged while running your race at your own pace. Have you ever heard the statement, "keeping up with the Joneses?" It's the same idea; don't run to keep up with others on this earth. Run your race to complete the call on your life, so that God's will on this earth intertwined with your assignment and purpose will come forth. You will get to the finish line unless you drop out of the race. Running guarantees you to cross the finish line, no matter the order or place in which you cross it.

—*No pain, no gain.*

Don't focus on how much further up the mountain you have to climb, focus on how far up the mountain you've already climbed. God is good; he has brought you this far to keep you, not to leave you. Take one step at a time! Living a Christian life is a work in progress daily. Although some days may be painful as you face mountains of problems and issues, there is life in God and the gain is good. Don't let the Devil's schemes and distractions sway your walk. His active plan is real to deter you, but seek God every step up the mountain.

——*"...so I will be with you; I will never leave nor forsake you."*

——*Joshua 1:5*

— "Get right or get left."

—*"wise men"*

It's a simple statement, yet it means so much. We have to get right in our salvation to have eternal life. There is no other option but through him Christ Jesus. If you go the alternative route, death in Hell is guaranteed.

It's biblical, not an opinion.

"My salvation and my honor depend on God; he is my mighty rock, my refuge."

—*Psalm 62:7*

—"*When it's God, it's good.*"

"For God is not a God of disorder but of peace."

—1 Corinthians 14:33

There aren't any shortages of blessings in Christ. If you're struggling with a decision, look at where the root of the decision originated. Is it a good place or a bad place? God does not give you a "bad" idea. Confusing decisions are simply rooted in the evil one and are too heavy and bleak to make the solid choice. Think about it, pray about it, sleep on it, but get peace before deciding. Remember to reflect over some past decisions and know the good ones are those of God.

Say to yourself, favor please find me today, and every day in what I need, desire, and want. When God can, he will.

Better yet, be a *Favor Finder* today.

—*The dash of your life: birth date—end date.*

Yes, we have to face the fact that we don't control our end or beginning, but what we can do is enhance our life by being strategic about what we do to live a full and appointed life in between our birth date and final resting date. Some say sunrise to sunset, but you get the idea. Live purposefully and be intentional about your everyday life. If you don't design your day, your day is defaulted to time stealers. Time stealers can come in the form of well-intended distractions such as things that can be done on weekends as well as after business hours in the day. You see time stealers could be you leisurely surfing on Facebook, Twitter, and other media sources throughout the day.

What comprises your dash in between your beginning to your end date is up to you. While we may not control when we enter this world or leave this natural world, we do maximize the opportunity to tailor our choices. How you spend that dash is truly a result of daily options, choices and selections by yours truly: *you*. Your assignment in life must become your passion. Otherwise, your life outcome may be encumbered by many unforeseen and uncomfortable experiences like Jonah's.

—Jonah 1:17

—"Work the Word, so the Word will work for you."

Read God's Word. Familiarize yourself with his promises, what God says about salvation, healing, and his will for your life. Have you tried to work your own miracles only for calamity to surface? Have you tried working the Word, so the Word will work for you? God is there as the primary source that distributes all the resources we need on this earth. Do your part first, work the Word because it will work for you. Read, pray and seek God's Word for your daily resources.

He's the primary source for all resources, as long as you're plugged in; you can get your power. Without plugging in to the source, you're bound to give out of power and lose sight.

Find out what the Word says and confess what it says about you and any situation you face. Seek God and speak his Word.

——Trusting God means to walk in faith.

—*Take the blinders off.*

"Immediately, something like scales fell from Saul's eyes, and he could see again."

—*Acts 9:18*

Sun glasses are designed to block out sunrays and help protect the eyes from unhealthy sun rays. Just as they are designed to protect the eyes, at times the blinders are inappropriate and need to come off because the vision may be slightly impaired from seeing the real thing.

God is needed in all aspects of life and requires that we seek him for direction in every aspect of life. When this is not the case, we are blinded by the light and unable to decipher truth from the fake in many aspects of life. Ask God to remove the scales from your eyes as he did for Saul in the Bible, so that you will be able to see without the blinders what God has for you. Seek him diligently for divine revelation, visions, dreams, etc.

When you take off the blinders, you can see through the *FOG: Favor of God*!

—Draw near to God for help.

"Come near to God and he will come near to you."

—James 4:8

—Say to yourself, "I wear the fragrance of favor."

Everyone listens to voices, either one or the other:

God or the Devil

Flesh or the Spirit

Which will you choose?

Surely when you hear God's voice, do what he says.

"So, as the Holy Spirit says: Today, if you hear his voice, do not harden your hearts as you did in the rebellion, during the time of testing in the desert."

——*Hebrews 3:7-8*

When Satan tells you lies about yourself, don't sign for the package; RTS (return to sender) his nonsense and accept the package God has for you. Choose life, not death.

——Choose light instead of darkness.

—Listen to his voice, it's real.

"Whether you turn to the right or to the left, your ears will hear a voice behind you, saying "This is the way; walk in it. He will also send you rain for the seed you sow in the ground, and the food that comes from the land will be rich and plentiful."

—Isaiah 30:21, 23

—"We can't do worldly things expecting Word results."

"You do not have, because you do not ask God. When you ask, you do not receive, because you ask with wrong motives, that you may spend what you get on your pleasures. You adulterous people, don't you know that friendship with the world is hatred toward God? Anyone who chooses to be a friend of the world becomes an enemy of God."
—*James 4:3-4*

Have you ever wondered why some things we desire never come to pass? It could be that we are making decisions to do worldly things with the expectation of receiving the promises of God from his Word; that is not how it works. The pleasures mentioned could be as simple as you wanting worldly possessions just for show from God, yet your motives demonstrate a selfish heart that gloats and is vain with what God has the ability to grant us overnight. Do a heart check up and ask yourself what you will do with Word results that need not be connected to worldly results.

—"Do what you can and God will do what you can't. Do the natural so that God can do the supernatural."

—wise men

You want to know how to get some things accomplished that seem impossible? Do what you can, so God can do what you can't. It's logical to think that we are limited in our human strength and solely reliant on God's supernatural to take us far beyond our limitations.

"With man this is impossible, but with God all things are possible."

—Matthew 19:26

—Be saved

"That if you confess with your mouth, 'Jesus is Lord,' and believe in your heart that God raised him from the dead, your will be saved. For it is with your heart that you believe and are justified, and it is with your mouth that you confess and are saved."

—Romans 10:9-10

—If you have a choice, choose what is right.

"If you do what is right, will you not be accepted? But if you do not do what is right, sin is crouching at your door; it desires to have you, but you must master it."

—Genesis 4:7

—Set the tone of your day, so that the enemy doesn't set the tone of your day for you.

—*Did you get his call?*

God has your gifts, talents, and abilities for greatness waiting for you. Accept the call if he's called you; accept the assignment if he's shown you what it is, but more importantly, accept him, the Son and Holy Spirit. They are a magnificent trinity.

"God's gifts and his call are irrevocable."

—*Romans 11:29*

—"*Be still and k**NO**w*"

"Be still, and know that I am God: I will be exalted among the heathen, I will be exalted in the earth."

—*Psalms 46:10 KJV*

When you don't know what to do, and you've done everything you can, trust God and rest in him. The scripture tells us to "be still and know that I am God." I would go as far as saying "be still and NO." That would be *no* to stressing, *no* to worrying, and *no* to trying within your human ability to take God's place, so yes, I say the word *NO*. *No* could also mean not now. Especially if whatever you desire has you worried, stressing, anxious, or reluctant to be still and rest in God. Psalms 46:10 is a directive from God to be *still* (rest) and *know* (no) that I am God. God is able when you're not. He has you covered but you first have to believe.

— *"Fight"*

Forgive

Ignite your passion

Give thanks for God's goodness

Hear the Holy Spirit's voice

Trust in God

When you make the choice to forgive and walk in full salvation, don't be surprised if the devil tempts and fights you on many levels. Fight back because the Word tells us that it is like a double-edged sword.

"For the word of God is alive and active. Sharper than any **double-edged sword**, it penetrates even to dividing soul and spirit, joints and marrow; it judges the thoughts and attitudes of the heart."

—*Hebrews 4:12*

Chapter 6: Seeds to Go

"A farmer went out to sow his seed. As he was scattering the seed, some fell along the path, and the birds came and ate it up. Some fell on rocky places, where it did not have much soil. It sprang up quickly, because the soil was shallow. But when the sun came up, the plants were scorched, and they withered because they had no root. Other seed fell among thorns, which grew up and choked the plants. Still other seed fell on good soil, where it produced a crop —a hundred, sixty or thirty times what was sown. He, who has ears, let him hear."

—*Matthew 13:3-9*

Discover what type of seeds you have by reading further in Matthew 13:18-23.

—Don't leave home without your armor.

The devil is always waiting.

The Armor of God

"Finally, be strong in the Lord and in his mighty power. Put on the full armor of God, so that you can take your stand against the devil's schemes. For our struggle is not against flesh and blood, but against the rulers, against the authorities, against the powers of this dark world and against the spiritual forces of evil in the heavenly realms. Therefore put on the full armor of God, so that when the day of evil comes, you may be able to stand your ground, and after you have done everything, to stand. Stand firm then, with the belt of truth buckled around your waist, with the breastplate of righteousness in place, and with your feet fitted with the readiness that comes from the gospel of peace. In addition to all this, take up the shield of faith, with which you can extinguish all the flaming arrows of the evil one. Take the helmet of salvation and the sword of the Spirit, which is the word of God. And pray in the Spirit on all occasions with all kinds of prayers and requests. With this in mind, be alert and always keep on praying for all the Lord's people."

—Ephesians 6:10-18 (NIV)

—Night versus day.

You ever heard someone perhaps refer to a set of twins, siblings, a couple or two friends as "night and day?"

God is light ← →Satan is Darkness

You can see in the light   Satan's deceptive ways
                            keeps you blinded to the
                            light.

If you are walking in the light, then congratulations to you. If not, please exchange the blinders for the light. I can assure you that you will not be disappointed.

In life you will either wait for it to happen or make it happen. Results or excuses -- which are you seeking? A guarantee is that you're seeking a set of excuses if you don't seek results immediately.

Note the seasons of life in a year:

Winter

Spring

Summer

Fall

Do/ Due

Do something starting today. It is due season for your change.

Be a sower and plant the right seeds in the lives of others you touch daily. Water your own seeds as well that have been planted within you. Guard, water, but most importantly, believe that your seeds have been planted in good soil and on good ground. What you sow is what you'll reap. Remember *all* things are possible in God, not *some* things.

"With man this is impossible, but with God all things are possible."

—*Matthew 19:26*

Be blessed.

Special Acknowledgements

"Mommy" (Ms. N. Smith)

V. Smith, Sr.

Charity Tarrence

Ceola Evans

Jacklyn Lavender

Sandra Ballard

Dawn Maye

Neva Alexander

Tracey Boss

Isreal Minkins

Sonya, Valerie, & Ms. Ruth Waddell

Rhonda Novak

Liliana Perez

Lois Bolton

King Williams

Many have sown seeds in my life. However, these ***extraordinary people*** that I acknowledge have done so during bleak moments and times as I wrote *Seeds of Hope*. I love, thank and wish you only God's best every day in what you do!

Meet the Author

Felicia holds a Bachelor's of Science degree in Psychology and Christian Counseling from Liberty University and is currently studying to become a Licensed Marriage and Family Therapist.

Smith is the Founder of the *Relate-2-Clinic*.

As an active Author of titles such as *Through The Eyes of A Daughter: Fathers, We Need You*, as well as other books, Columnist Writer for Empower Magazine, coach, speaker, and professional, Felicia's mission is to work to promote sound mental health of individuals.

Queen Dream Publishing invites you to contact us for additional copies of this book and for the Author's speaking availability at your upcoming event. For more information about Queen Dream Publishing or for your comments and responses to this book, contact us by writing or emailing at the addresses below.

Email: info@queendreamz.com

www.queendreamz.com

3961 Floyd Road, Suite 300-274, Austell, GA 30106.

www.ingramcontent.com/pod-product-compliance
Lightning Source LLC
Chambersburg PA
CBHW030220170426
43194CB00007BA/805